RN AIRCRAFT CARRIERS

Cdr David Hobbs MBE RN (Retd)

INTRODUCTION

Aircraft carriers were invented by the Royal Navy and, in the 90 years since the first examples went to sea, it has done more than any other Service to improve the technology that has allowed increasingly sophisticated aircraft to be operated far from home or friendly overseas bases. In addition to these facts, Britain has exported more aircraft carriers to other navies than any other nation.

The term aircraft carrier, however, does not adequately describe the capability of the particular vessel in question and applies equally to the 1924 HERMES of 13,700 tons and the 1951 EAGLE of 49,950 tons. Nor does it specify the role or roles in which a carrier might be operating. These could be as diverse as strike warfare, fleet air defence, sea control, amphibious assault or anti-submarine warfare. Carriers have frequently been used in secondary roles including the movement of military and air forces to trouble spots, disaster relief and the peacetime duty of 'showing the flag'.

This is not intended to be an operational history but, rather to provide illustrations of a number of British and Commonwealth aircraft carriers, by no means all, performing a range of tasks that illustrate their capabilities between 1918 and 1985.
I hope you enjoy reading through it as much as I enjoyed putting this book together.

David Hobbs

Twyford, November 2008

HMS FURIOUS was designed as a light battle cruiser with a main armament of two single 18-inch guns, one in a turret forward and one aft. Following recommendations from the Grand Fleet Aircraft Committee, she was actually completed with a flight deck and hangar forward. Fighters and reconnaissance aircraft could take off on their wheeled undercarriages but they were not expected to be able to land back on. Shortly after her completion, however, on 2 August 1917, Squadron Commander Dunning DSC RNAS landed a Sopwith Pup on the deck. This was the first time in history that an operational fighter had landed on an operational warship. In consequence she was modified again with a landing deck over a second hangar aft, but turbulence and funnel smoke from the central superstructure made landing dangerous, hence the rope barrier to stop aircraft from crashing into the funnel. She is seen here in the disruptive pattern paint scheme she wore for the attack on Tondern in 1918, the first successful carrier-borne strike on enemy installations ashore by any navy.   *(Author's Collection)*

4

HMS VINDICTIVE was laid down as the name ship of the 'Cavendish' class cruisers but re-named in honour of the ship that played a key role in the Zeebrugge Raid in 1918. She was the third fast carrier to be completed for the Grand Fleet after FURIOUS and ARGUS and, like the former, had a "flying off deck" forward and a landing on deck aft of a central bridge and funnel structure. After the failure of the FURIOUS deck landing trials and the success of those in ARGUS she seldom operated aircraft but did ferry RAF units for operations against the Bolsheviks in North Russia in 1919. Reputedly her after deck was less prone to turbulence than that of FURIOUS and at least one successful landing was carried out by a Sopwith Pup in November 1918. She was converted back into a cruiser in 1923 but retained the forward hangar and was later used for catapult trials.

(Author's Collection)

HMS ARGUS in the 'dazzle' paint scheme in which she was completed in September 1918. The scheme was designed by the famous marine artist Norman Wilkinson who took the view that there was no future in trying to conceal warships with camouflage paint. Rather, his intention was to confuse or dazzle enemy optical range-takers and cause an incorrect assessment of heading, both effects leading to errors of aim in a gunnery fire-control solution. The scheme was viewed with caution by the Admiralty but applied to ARGUS, LONDON and a number of cruisers, escorts and merchant ships. Whilst it made the ships more visible, there is evidence to suggest that the scheme worked in practice. ARGUS was the world's first effective, flush-decked aircraft carrier. Originally laid down for an Italian shipping line, her incomplete hull was purchased by the Admiralty for conversion to an aircraft carrier in order to save building time. Her first aircraft were Sopwith T 1 torpedo planes and 2 F1 'Ship's Camel' fighters with which, had the Great War continued for a few more days, she would have launched an attack on the German High Seas Fleet in its harbours, pre-dating the famous Japanese attack on the US fleet in Pearl Harbour by 23 years.

(Author's Collection)

The incomplete HMS EAGLE in the English Channel in 1920 carrying out sea trials to validate the concept of the starboard side island. Note that she has only one funnel and a temporary mast. The first aircraft to land on was a Sopwith 2 F1 Camel and 143 landings were eventually completed by a variety of aircraft types. She had been laid down as the battleship ALMIRANTE COCHRANE for Chile in 1913 but was requisitioned by the Admiralty for conversion into an aircraft carrier during the First World War. Her sister ship ALMIRANTE LATORRE was requisitioned as a battleship when further advanced in construction and served as a battleship with the Grand Fleet at Jutland as HMS CANADA before being returned to Chile after the war. Following Admiralty approval to complete her for trials, EAGLE raised steam for the first time in March 1920. After their successful conclusion, she was completed as an aircraft carrier in 1924. *(Author's Collection)*

HMS HERMES was the first ship in the world to be designed and built from the outset to operate aircraft although the concept transformed through several evolutions before she was completed. The after lift opened aft onto the quarterdeck as well as into the single hangar forward and was originally intended to allow the operation of seaplanes. The 'hump' at the after end of the flight deck was originally the rear anchor point for the system of fore and aft wires but was retained after their removal as it was believed to smooth the airflow in the landing area. She was built by Armstrong Whitworth on the Tyne but towed to Devonport Dockyard for completion after being launched in 1919. The photograph shows her carrying out steaming trials in Plymouth Sound during 1923 before being commissioned for operational service.
(Ken Kelly)

HMS FURIOUS operating in the 1930s. The doors from the upper hangar onto the slip flight deck are open and two Fly-catchers are lined up ready to take off. They have been protected by the wind-break which is being lowered to let them launch. The steam shown aft of the lowered forward lift shows that the ship is already into wind but not moving fast as no great wind over the deck was needed to launch aircraft as light as the Flycatcher. Note the soot stains at the after end of the flight deck where smoke was exhausted when not at flying stations, known as 'smoking up'. At flying stations it was ex-hausted from the black painted ship's side lower down, known as 'smoking down'. *(Author's Collection)*

HMS COURAGEOUS in Plymouth Sound soon after her completion as an aircraft carrier in 1928. She subsequently deployed to the Mediterranean Fleet and, on 18 October 1929, her aircraft performed the first flying display to be seen over Istanbul. Note that the door from the upper hangar onto the 'slip' flight deck is open, designed to allow fighters to take off directly from the hangar when the main flight deck was crowded with aircraft. In practice the capability was impractical and seldom used. The prominent netting visible aft of the island was intended to prevent the lightly loaded biplanes of the period from being blown over the side as the ship turned out of wind after a recovery since a gust could generate sufficient velocity to lift unlashed aircraft!

(Author's Collection)

Between the two World Wars, HERMES spent a number of years on the China Station. She is seen her anchored off Wei-Hei-Wei operating Fairey IIIF seaplanes. Before 1939 all British carrier-borne aircraft were designed to operate either with wheels or floats and the ships carried the equipment necessary to convert them. The awnings were unusual for a carrier, designed to protect personnel working on the flight deck from the sun while the ship had no forward motion. The big crane aft of the island is lifting the aircraft from the deck park onto the sea, from where they will take off. This concept of operations provided a temporary base from which patrols could be flown but failed to make adequate use of the carrier's inherent mobility and flexibility.

(Author's Collection)

HMS EAGLE in 1933 painted in the China Station paint scheme of white hull with buff island and masts. Her original battleship hull is still evident under the added structure of the flight deck and island. The enormous spotting top on the fore mast was intended to control the nine 6-inch Mk XVII guns. These were to enable the ship to defend herself against enemy cruisers, a legacy from the original design concept when it was assumed that she would scout ahead of the battle fleet where she might be intercepted herself by enemy scouting forces.

(Author's Collection)

From 1920 to 1925, FURIOUS was converted to a through-deck carrier with two hangars served by 'T' shaped lifts so that aircraft could be struck down before their wings were folded. In the Second World War this feature allowed her to operate the early Seafires with greater ease than the later carriers with their small lifts. Surprisingly, she did not have an island and funnel gases were trunked aft either side of the hangar to exhaust at the rear of the flight deck. Note the black paint aft to avoid smoke stains on the grey paint. She is seen here, between the wars, anchored off Invergordon in the Cromarty Firth with ships of the Atlantic Fleet.

(Ken Kelly)

HMS EAGLE (1) at sea off Gibraltar. Prior to the entry into service of the Invincible class in 1980, she was to only British aircraft carrier to be completed with two funnels.

(Author's Collection)

HMS GLORIOUS anchored off the breakwater lighthouse in Plymouth Sound during 1935. She was another light battle cruiser conversion and had re-commissioned as an aircraft carrier in 1930. She had just completed a refit in Devonport in which she was fitted with arrester gear and catapults and was about to re-join the Mediterranean Fleet. The canvas 'box' hinged out to port of the island was the flying control position, the predecessor of the modern 'flyco', from which Commander 'Air' controlled ranging and launching. It was not put out for aircraft landings for obvious reasons and when not in use it was hinged back against the island. The box like structures at the forward end of the flight deck were the ends of the newly fitted catapult mechanisms.

(Author's Collection)

EAGLE (1) in 1935 after modernisation. She had no arrester wires at this stage, with aircraft relying on their brakes to stop after landing onto a clear deck with no deck park or barrier. To speed things up, aircraft were taxied straight onto the T-shaped forward lift and struck down with wings spread, to be folded subsequently in the hangar. The lift was designed to move quickly as the next aircraft could not land on until it was back at flight deck level. The after lift did not need to be T-shaped as it was used to range aircraft relatively more slowly. There was no landing safety officer, or 'batsman' and pilots judged their own landings. Note the palisades, or large nets, on the flight deck edge to port of the forward lift designed to stop aircraft being blown over the side at the end of their landing run, before handlers could grasp them.

(*Author's Collection*)

The original caption to this photograph read "*HMS Glorious and her fighting squadron*". The aircraft are Fairey Swordfish of 825 NAS, the first unit to be equipped with them in July 1936 and GLORIOUS was their first carrier. The white circle painted on the flight deck was intended to show pilots the ideal touch-down point in the days before deck landing control officers or 'batsmen'. One Swordfish is neatly lined up to 'hit' the mark. GLORIOUS was sunk on 8 June 1940 by gunfire from SCHARNHORST and GNEISENAU while ferrying RAF fighters back to the UK from Norway. *(Author's Collection)*

HMS COURAGEOUS in the Cromarty Firth off Invergordon during autumn exercises after joining the Home Fleet in 1936.
(*Syd Goodman Collection*)

HMS EAGLE alongside Devonport Dockyard on 14 July 1936 on completion of a refit during which arrester wires were fitted, stowage for air weapons was increased and flight deck lighting was installed to allow night flying. Extra close-range anti-
aircraft weapons were also fitted.
(Syd Goodman Collection)

HMS ARK ROYAL (III) anchored at Spithead on 16 June 1939. Although she was completed more than six months earlier, the two port side pom-pom mountings have yet to be fitted and their sponsons, just above the three Carley floats are empty. The 'ARK' had a short but famous wartime career before being sunk by a single torpedo from U-81 on 14 November 1941. She saw action with the Home Fleet in the North Sea and throughout the Norwegian Campaign of 1940 after which she joined Force H based on Gibraltar with which she saw action against French and Italian forces in the Western Mediterranean. On 26 May 1941 one of her Swordfish hit BISMARCK's rudder with a torpedo, preventing her from escaping to an Axis port in France and enabling her to be brought to action by battleships of the Home Fleet. *(Author's Collection)*

ARK ROYAL (III), seen here steaming into wind, launching a range of Hawker Ospreys and Fairey Swordfish in 1938 or early 1939. The low wind over the deck, shown by the funnel smoke and the low ship speed shown by the bow wave emphasise how relatively simple the lightweight biplanes of the day were to launch. The three lighter rectangles on deck are lifts, sited just forward, alongside and just aft of the island. They were unusual in that each had two platforms, serving the two hangars which were one on top of the other. Thus it took two moves to get an aircraft from the flight deck to the lower hangar, each platform serving only one deck. The lower hull was armoured to cruiser standards and the main belt can be seen just aft of the lowest row of scuttles; unlike subsequent carriers, the flight deck and hangar sides were not armoured, allowing double the number of aircraft to be carried. Her loss in 1941 was due, partially, to bad design as there were no diesel generators to provide power if steam was lost and partially to poor damage control procedures by the ship's company.

(Author's Collection)

HMS COURAGEOUS seen dressed overall during a Royal visit to the mobilised reserve fleet at Weymouth on 9 August 1939. Days later she formed part of the Task Force that escorted the British Expeditionary Force to France and on 16 September she sailed from Devonport with four destroyers to carry out anti-submarine patrols in the Atlantic with the Swordfish aircraft of 811 and 822 NAS embarked. On 17 September she was sunk by torpedoes from U-29 in the South West Approaches, losing 518 men including the Commanding Officer, out of a complement 1,260.

(Ken Kelly)

In 1939 HMS HERMES re-commissioned from the Reserve Fleet for operational service. Her small flight deck is seen to advantage with the wind-break forward lowered flush with the deck. The 'T'-shaped lifts were designed to allow aircraft to be struck down into the hangar while their wings were still spread to clear the deck quickly for the next landing.

(Syd Goodman Collection)

Another view of HERMES in 1939, note the two-digit flight deck recognition letters common at the time. Two of the Swordfish are camouflaged; the other two are still in their pre-war silver finish. *(Syd Goodman Collection)*

HMS GLORIOUS photographed on 26 May 1940 from an escorting destroyer. The aircraft ranged on deck and running are Hawker Hurricanes of 46 Squadron, Royal Air Force. The ship is accelerating and turning into wind to fly them off to Skaanland in Norway where they were to re-fuel before flying on to Bardufoss. When it was decided to evacuate Norway, the Hurricanes landed on GLORIOUS on 7 June, the first time that high-performance monoplanes had landed on a British carrier.

(*Author's Collection*)

A poor quality image but one of the last photographs taken of GLORIOUS before she was sunk by the battle-cruisers SCHARNHORST and GNEISENAU on 8 June 1940. Note the disruptive pattern camouflage she wore at this stage of the Norwegian Campaign. The lack of aircraft visible on deck would indicate that it was probably taken after 1 June while she waited off the Norwegian coast to embark RAF fighters for evacuation to the UK. (*Author's Collection*)

HMS INDOMITABLE was the fourth unit of the 'Illustrious' group, built to a modified design that worked a lower 'half hangar' under the original and made many other detail improvements including greater stowage for aircraft fuel. A larger forward lift allowed aircraft such as the Sea Hurricane with non-folding wings to be struck down into the upper hangar. The photograph shows her shortly after completion in a disruptive pattern paint scheme. The 'dustbin' shaped object on the tripod mast is a Type 72 aircraft homing beacon.

(Author's Collection)

One of the last photographs taken of the 'old' HERMES before she was sunk by Japanese naval aircraft off Batticaloa in Ceylon on 9 April 1942. She had been ordered to clear Trincomalee the day before because of an expected air raid from Admiral Nagumo's carrier task force. She had no aircraft embarked and relied on shore-based RAF fighters for protection which, in the event, failed to materialise. 307 officers and men were lost when she sank. *(Author's Collection)*

By 1942 HMS FURIOUS was fitted with a small island from which flying operations were controlled. The ship was still 'driven' from the original compass platform on the starboard deck edge forward. By then the forward flying-off deck was no longer useable and a twin 4-inch Mark XIX HA gun mounting has been installed on it. The 'dustbin' shaped object on the pole mast is a Type 72 aircraft homing beacon.

(Syd Goodman Collection)

HMS BEGUM was another 'Ruler' class escort carrier built from the outset as a warship but to a mercantile design in the USA. She was originally the USS BOLINAS and was provisionally named CHASTISER by the RN before she was commissioned as BEGUM in August 1943. She saw brief operational service carrying out anti-submarine sweeps in the Indian Ocean with the Avengers and Wildcats of 832 NAS embarked in 1944. She was used to ferry aircraft to Australia in 1945 and was returned to the USN in 1946.

(T. Ferrers-Walker)

HMS PRETORIA CASTLE was requisitioned from the Union Castle line by the Admiralty in 1939 and saw service as an armed merchant cruiser before being converted into a trials carrier by Swan Hunter in 1942. The work involved stripping her down to 'C' deck and then building her up again with a hangar, flight deck and island. Much of her equipment was experimental and she was the only British carrier to date fitted with a cordite-powered catapult. Apart from one operational deployment escorting convoys to and from Iceland, she spent her whole career carrying out flying trials in the Clyde areas. She was converted back into a cargo liner in 1946 and re-named WARWICK CASTLE. *(Author's Collection)*

In November 1942 the US Navy asked the Admiralty for the loan of an aircraft carrier to reinforce its depleted Pacific Fleet. HMS VICTORIOUS was refitted with USN equipment in Norfolk, Virginia and passed through the Panama Canal into the Pacific on 2 February 1943. She operated with USS SARATOGA as a task group with 882, 896 and 898 NAS embarked with Wildcat fighters and 832 NAS embarked with Avengers. Because of the RN's greater fighter direction experience, they frequently sailed with all the fighters in VICTORIOUS and all the strike aircraft in SARATOGA. The aircraft were all painted with USN style 'star' markings, the ship's company wore USN uniform with RN badges and the ship was painted in USN blue. The chefs even had to use USN style dried mashed potato when she ran out of real 'spuds'! She is seen here anchored with SARATOGA off Noumea in New Caledonia. VICTORIOUS returned to the UK for a refit in Liverpool in September 1943. *(Ken Kelly)*

Seafires of 899 NAS over HMS INDOMITABLE with others ranged ready for take-off at the after end of the flight deck. Both were products of the Vickers' engineering 'empire'. This photograph was used by the firm during the Second World War to publicise its production of weapons for the Royal Navy. INDOMITABLE was built at the Barrow-in-Furness Yard and completed in October 1941.

(Author's Collection)

MV RAPANA was a tanker MAC-Ship originally built in Holland but converted by Smith's Dock on the Tyne in 1943. In October 1943, her Swordfish of 836 NAS L Flight carried out an attack on a U-boat whilst escorting Convoy SC 143 but there were no signs to confirm a 'kill'. Like other MAC-Ships, she lost about 30% of the available cargo space when aircraft operating arrangements were installed. She was converted back into a tanker after the war and re-named ROTULA.

(*Author's Collection*)

HMS RAVAGER was an Attacker class escort carrier that spent most of her time with the Royal Navy operating as a deck landing training carrier based in the Clyde. She operated in the role, with small breaks, between July 1943 and December 1945. She is seen here turning out of wind after a recovery.

(*Author's Collection*)

A brand new and immaculately painted RAVAGER seen on the Willamette River shortly after her completion by the Seattle-Tacoma Shipbuilding Corporation in April 1943. Note that the camouflage on each side of the bow is different. On her delivery voyage to the UK in July she ferried the newly formed 846 NAS with its Avengers across the Atlantic.

(*Author's Collection*)

During January 1943 HMS ARGUS formed part of the escort for convoy KMF 8 from the Clyde to North Africa. She is seen here during that month with the after part of the hull painted black to hide the staining caused by funnel smoke exhausted from tunnels under the round-down at the after part of the flight deck. (*Syd Goodman Collection*)

Stern details of the escort carrier HMS BITER in March 1943 after she completed a refit to equip her for anti-submarine operations in the Western Approaches Command. She embarked 811 'composite' Naval Air Squadron with both Swordfish and Martlet aircraft. The single USN Mark 9 4-inch gun in its 'tub' aft is trained to port. *(Syd Goodman Collection)*

The camouflage scheme applied to HMS BITER is seen to good effect in this photograph taken in March 1943. She was originally laid down as the mercantile 49 but taken over, incomplete, by the USN in 1940 and completed as a unit of the Avenger class for the Royal Navy by the Atlantic Basin Iron Works in Brooklyn. *(Syd Goodman Collection)*

HMS TRACKER was laid down as the mercantile MORMACMAIL by the Seattle-Tacoma Shipbuilding Corporation but completed as the sixth escort carrier built in the USA for the Royal Navy in January 1943 as a unit of the Attacker class. Note how the camouflage paint scheme has been extended over the wooden flight deck. *(Syd Goodman Collection)*

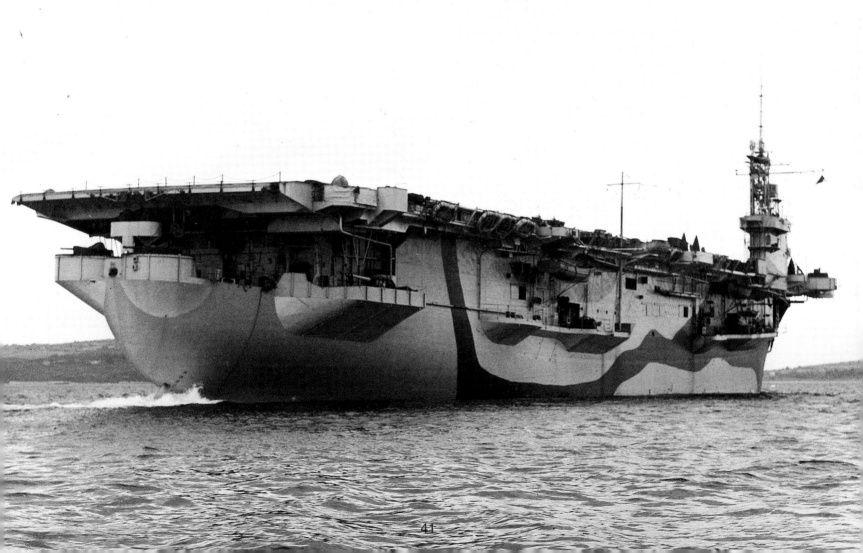

HMS TRACKER shortly after her completion in 1943. Despite their mercantile origins these were well-equipped and effective ships capable of operating the full range of allied carrier-borne aircraft. (*Syd Goodman Collection*)

HMS FENCER was an 'Attacker' class escort carrier built as the USS CROATAN but transferred to the Royal Navy in February 1943. She is seen here forming part of the Home Fleet task force that carried out the first carrier-borne strike on the battleship TIRPITZ in Kaa Fjord, Operation 'Tungsten'. The fleet carrier FURIOUS is visible in the background with another escort carrier beyond her. The Barracuda strike aircraft of 8 and 52 Torpedo Bomber Reconnaissance Wings were flown from FURIOUS and VICTORIOUS with fighter cover provided by aircraft from EMPEROR, PURSUER and SEARCHER. FENCER's task was to provide anti-submarine cover with the embarked Swordfish and Wildcats of 842 NAS.

(Author's Collection)

ILLUSTRIOUS (right) and the maintenance carrier UNICORN moored stern to stern in Trincomalee harbour whilst serving with the Eastern Fleet in 1944. The big opening under the after flight deck in UNICORN allowed aircraft to be moved from her upper hangar onto a lighter suspended from above and lowered into the water for transport ashore or to another ship. ILLUSTRIOUS arrived in Trincomalee in January 1944 and was one of the first ships to form part of the British Pacific Fleet later in the year. Her aircraft took part in the attacks on Palembang in January 1945 and in the Okinawa campaign in April.
(Ken Kelly)

IMPLACABLE anchored in the Clyde on 21 August 1944. She was one of the last two armoured carriers of the 'Illustrious' group. She was both larger and heavier than the earlier ships with two hangars, one over the other and four, rather than three shafts. To save top-weight, hangar height was reduced to 14 feet; a limitation that damned the ships for all of their short lives as it severely limited the types of aircraft that could be struck down. Modification after 1945 was considered and would have been possible but at a high cost, only fully appreciated when sister ship VICTORIOUS took eight years to modernise.

(Author's Collection)

An unusual view of HMS INDOMITABLE in dry dock in Bombay in June 1944. She was about to join the new British Pacific Fleet and had an air group comprising 5 Naval Fighter Wing with 1839 and 1844 NAS equipped with Hellcats and 12 Torpedo Bomber Reconnaissance Wing with 815 and 817 NAS equipped with Barracudas. The latter did not perform well in the high temperatures encountered in the Indian Ocean and were soon replaced by the Avengers of 857 NAS. Her first operation in the new theatre was a strike on Emmahaven (Sumatra) with VICTORIOUS in August 1944.

(Author's Collection)

HMS NAIRANA soon after her completion seen working up for operational service in the Clyde exercise areas in January 1944. Her small flight deck precluded a deck park of any useful size and the single lift aft made ranging aircraft from the forward end of the hangar difficult. Like other British-built escort carriers she was used on the Russian Convoy runs since it was believed that her riveted hull was less susceptible to cracking than the welded hulls of US-built ships. In March 1946 she was lent to the Royal Netherlands Navy as its first aircraft carrier and re-named KAREL DOORMAN. She was returned to the RN on 28 May 1948 and, purchase negotiations having been completed, the former 'Colossus' class light fleet carrier VENERABLE was handed over and re-commissioned as KAREL DOORMAN on the same day. *(Author's Collection)*

HMS RAJAH was a 'Ruler' class escort carrier which had been laid down as USS PRINCE but transferred under Lend/Lease arrangements and re-named before completion. Apart from a brief period carrying out deck landing training in the Clyde in August1944, she spent her whole career as a ferry carrier. In December she was allocated to USN operational control, complete with her RN ship's company, to ferry USN aircraft from San Diego to Pearl Harbour, returning to RN control in August 1945. After a period in use as a troopship, she was returned to the USN in December 1946 and sold for conversion to a merchant ship.

(Author's Collection)

The slipway in Devonport Dockyard in 1944 showing HMS TERRIBLE under construction, the only aircraft carrier ever to have been built in a Royal Dockyard. Like her five sister ships of the 'Majestic' class she never served with the Royal Navy but was, instead, purchased for the Royal Australian Navy on 3 June 1947 and commissioned as HMAS SYDNEY. The Admiralty planned, at one stage, to build a much larger carrier at Devonport and compulsorily purchased land to extend the building slip to over 1,000 feet. The project never came to anything and much of the land has since been handed back to the city.

(Author's Collection)

Merchant Aircraft Carriers, known as MAC-Ships, were wartime expedients intended to operate Swordfish aircraft for the anti-submarine defence of Atlantic convoys. A simple flight deck was constructed on top of a mercantile hull. Grain ships had a small hangar and could operate four aircraft, tankers had no hangar and could only operate three. In the latter case the aircraft had to stay out on deck in all weathers when not flying. This is AMASTRA, a tanker MAC-Ship converted for her new role by Smith's Dock in North Shields in 1943. The two Swordfish aft give scale to the tiny flight deck and landing with any sort of ship motion must have been an exciting experience. During a recovery, aircraft on deck would have been pushed forward of the barrier, visible in the lowered position, just forward of the island.

(*Author's Collection*)

EMPIRE MACALPINE was a grain carrier, converted into the first MAC-Ship while still under construction. In May 1943 Lieutenant Commander R Slater RN, the commanding officer of 836 NAS, landed a Swordfish on board; the first time that an aircraft had landed on a merchant ship. 836 NAS provided detachments for all the British MAC-Ships. MAC-Ships were manned by Merchant Navy crews; the RN provided the Air department, aircrew and maintainers and the ship's guns were manned by soldiers of the Defensively Equipped Merchant Ship Service (DEMS). Unlike the tanker MAC-Ships, grain carriers had no barrier as aircraft were kept in the hangar rather than in a deck park.

(Author's Collection).

The Attacker class escort carrier HUNTER streaming a buoyant hose to refuel the cruiser ROYALIST during Operation 'Outing', a series of strikes against German forces in the Aegean, during September 1944. HUNTER had the Seafire fighters of 807 NAS embarked at the time and, together with aircraft from SEARCHER, PURSUER and KHEDIVE, they caused considerable damage to enemy installations. Note the use of semaphore to pass secure tactical communications between the ships at short range.   (*Author's Collection*)

The brand new IMPLACABLE anchored in the Clyde during August 1944. Although she had just started her work-up, the camouflage paint forward had already taken quite a battering from the rough seas encountered.

(*Author's Collection*)

HMS FENCER photographed on 29 June 1944 while taking part in Operation 'Wanderers', a U-boat hunt off the Norwegian Coast with 842 and 881 Naval Air Squadrons embarked. She operated in company with STRIKER, the cruiser SHEFFIELD and 6 destroyers with the intention of simulating either an Arctic convoy or an allied landing in Norway, forcing the enemy to retain significant forces in the area.

(*Syd Goodman Collection*)

HMS FORMIDABLE at Scapa Flow on 9 June 1944 while serving with the Home Fleet. During 1943 she had been re-fitted in Belfast, a number of new close-range anti-aircraft weapons were fitted including the four 20mm Oerlikons visible under the round-down.

(Syd Goodman Collection)

Another ship of the large 'Ruler' class, HMS EMPRESS was built as the USS CARNEGIE but loaned to the Royal Navy from June 1943. Defect rectification after completion took a long time and she saw no active service until she joined the 21st Aircraft Carrier Squadron in the East Indies Fleet in 1945. She operated both Hellcats and Avengers in strikes against Japanese installations in Malaya, Sumatra and the Nicobar and Andaman Islands. She was present at the re-occupation of Singapore in September 1945, with 896 NAS Hellcats embarked, and visited Wellington in New Zealand in November. EMPRESS was returned to the USN and broken up for scrap in 1946. *(Author's Collection)*

The 'Ruler' class escort carrier HMS AMEER under way with Hellcats of 804 NAS on deck. She was commissioned as USS BAFFINS in June 1943 and transferred to the Royal Navy at Vancouver a month later under Lend/Lease arrangements. During 1944 she carried out a series of strike operations with the East Indies Fleet, based in Trincomalee. In one of them, Operation 'Livery', Hellcat fighters from AMEER and EMPEROR flew more than 150 sorties and destroyed over 30 enemy aircraft on the ground. She was narrowly missed by the only 'Kamikaze' attack on British warships to be mounted in the Bay of Bengal and was later returned to the USN in January 1946.   *(Author's Collection)*

HMS FORMIDABLE returning to Sydney in company with IMPLACABLE on 24 August 1945. She had a long and hard war culminating with the British Pacific Fleet as flagship of Rear Admiral Sir Philip Vian, flag officer 1st Aircraft Carrier Squadron. Only days before, on 9 August 1945 Lieutenant R H Grey DSC RCNVR, Senior Pilot of 1841 NAS, was awarded a posthumous Victoria Cross for leading an attack from her against Japanese warships in Onagawa Wan. FORMIDABLE was the second ship of the 'Illustrious' class to be completed and suffered extensive damage from bombs and Kamikaze hits in the Mediterranean and the Far East during her wartime service. After a number of trooping runs between Australia and the UK in 1946 she paid off into un-maintained reserve at Spithead. *(Author's Collection)*

HMS GLORY was built by Harland and Wolff in Belfast and was the fourth light fleet carrier to be completed. She arrived in Sydney too late to see action but earned a place in history when the surrender of all Japanese forces in New Britain to General B A H Sturdee of the Australian Army took place on her flight deck on 6 September 1945, near Rabaul. A brass plaque, unfortunately lost when GLORY was scrapped, marked the spot on the flight deck where the event took place.

(Author's Collection)

HM Ships IMPLACABLE and FORMIDABLE passing through the boom into Sydney Harbour on 24 August 1945, returning from operations off Japan. With the sudden end to the war in the Far East which had been expected to last for another year at least, most minds on board were no doubt thinking of the 'run ashore' to come. Few photographs have survived of anti-submarine booms in operation. *(Author's Collection)*

HMS IMPLACABLE on 24 August 1945 when she returned to Sydney from operations off Japan with FORMIDABLE. Having been the last fleet carrier to join the British Pacific Fleet, she stayed in the Far East after the end of the war and toured Australia and New Zealand in 1946. After her return to the UK, she became flagship of the Home Fleet with an air group that comprised 801 NAS with Sea Hornets, 813 NAS with Firebrands and 815 NAS with Barracudas. She often embarked Sea Vampire jet fighters of 702 NAS, the jet fighter evaluation unit with considerable success. After a period as a training ship, IMPLACABLE paid off in 1954 when she was only ten years old. She was scrapped in 1955.   *(Author's Collection)*

In the immediate aftermath of World War 2, allied troops and former Prisoners of War had to be ferried over large distances in considerable numbers. The British Pacific Fleet used its carriers for the task in the autumn of 1945 as their large hangars, accommodation and decks were ideal for the task. This photograph shows HMS IMPLACABLE arriving in Sydney Harbour on 15 November 1945 having ferried 2,126 soldiers of the 7th Australian Division from Balik Papan in Borneo, together with a number of their vehicles and guns, secured on the flight deck. Whilst on passage she had passed through the Prince of Wales' Channel in the Torres Straits at the tip of Cape York in Northern Queensland. She was, at that time, the largest ship ever to do so and for the next three days she sailed down the east coast of Australia inside the Great Barrier Reef, giving her 'passengers' a memorable cruise.

(Author's Collection)

HMS REAPER was another 'Ruler' class ship used as a ferry carrier. Her original name was USS WINJAH and she was transferred to the RN at Tacoma Shipyard in February 1944 under Lend/Lease arrangements. She was in turn lent back to USN operational control, with her ship's company, in January 1945 and is seen here ferrying USN aircraft from San Diego to Pearl Harbour en route to the Pacific Fleet carriers on 29 April 1945. Densely packed on the flight deck like this and in the hangar, these ships could ferry as many as 90 aircraft at a time. *(Author's Collection)*

HMS VENERABLE on 1 May 1945. She was completed by Cammell Laird at Birkenhead on 17 January, one of the first four units of the 'Colossus' class to join the fleet. She arrived in Sydney on 22 July 1945 too late for operations with the British Pacific Fleet but was present at the Surrender of Hong Kong in August, flying strike against 'diehard' kamikaze units on 31 August. She remained in the Far East until February 1947 and, after her return to the UK, she was sold to the Dutch Government and re-named KAREL DOORMAN after the admiral who had commanded allied ships at the Battle of the Java Sea.

(Author's Collection)

A port side view of VENERABLE in May 1945 working up off Malta prior to service with the British Pacific Fleet. She was commissioned as HNethMS KAREL DOORMAN on 28 May 1948 and served with the Dutch Navy for twenty years, being extensively re-built with an angled deck and steam catapult between 1954 and 1958. She operated a variety of aircraft types including Sea Furies, Sea Hawks, Fireflies and Trackers. After a serious engine room fire, she was repaired in 1968 and sold to Argentina with the new name 25 de MAYO. During the South Atlantic War in 1982 she sortied against the British Task Force with Super Etendards and Skyhawks embarked but the torpedoing of the cruiser GENERAL BELGRANO by the British submarine CONQUEROR led to her returning to port and she played no further part in the war; her aircraft operated from ashore.

(Author's Collection)

Hands fallen in and aircraft in an Alpha Range on INDEFATIGABLE's flight deck ready for a ceremonial entry into Melbourne for a fleet visit in January 1946. She is painted in the immediate post-war scheme with the lower half of the hull in dark grey and the upper half and island in light grey. The visit was a big success and is still remembered by many British Pacific Fleet veterans who were lucky enough to be there. *(Author's Collection)*

The 1st Aircraft Carrier Squadron, comprising ILLUSTRIOUS, FORMIDABLE, INDOMITABLE, VICTORIOUS and INDE-FATIGABLE formed part of the British Pacific Fleet that operated with the USN during Operation 'Iceberg' the landings on Okinawa in April 1945. INDOMITABLE is seen here anchored in San Pedro Bay, part of Leyte Gulf in the Philippine Islands for a replenishment period half way through the operation after 32 days at sea, the longest a British fleet had remained at sea continuously since the days of sail. Replacement aircraft were provided from the Fleet Air Maintenance Group in UNICORN during this period. Note the cruisers in the distant background which give some idea of the enormous distances that the ship's boat routine had to cover in the Bay.

(Author's Collection)

The deck landing training role meant that RAVAGER had to embark examples of every type of operational aircraft for student pilots to use during their qualifying deck landings. This view of the hangar shows a mixture of night-fighter Fulmars, a Wildcat, Avengers and Barracudas in 1945. Note the overhead hoist system for component removal and the spotless deck.
(*Author's Collection*)

HMS OCEAN is seen here shortly after her completion, just too late for war service. She was equipped as a night-fighter carrier and had a USN supplied SM-1 radar over the bridge rather than the standard but less effective British Type 277 fitted to her sister ships. She spent her first few months in commission as a trials ship and successfully recovered the first jet to land on an aircraft carrier deck in December 1945.

(Syd Goodman Collection)

HMS PIONEER was laid down as the light fleet carrier MARS of the Colossus class in 1942 but was converted to a maintenance carrier and re-named before completion. She could not operate fixed-wing aircraft and so the anti-aircraft armament was mounted on the upper deck rather than on sponsons. She served with the British Pacific Fleet in 1945 but paid off into reserve on return to the UK in 1946 and saw no further service. *(Syd Goodman Collection)*

In May 1945 HMS VENERABLE was working up to operational efficiency off Malta using RNAS Hal Far as a diversion air-field. The two aircraft on deck are Barracudas. (*Syd Goodman Collection*)

HMS VENGEANCE in 1945 with the Corsairs of 1850 and Barracudas of 812 Naval Air squadrons embarked. She was just too late to see action, having sailed from Sydney for her first operational sortie on 15 August 1945 - VJ Day. She was present at the re-occupation of Hong Kong with other ships of the British Pacific Fleet.   (*Syd Goodman Collection*)

'Up Channel Night.' HMS INDEFATIGABLE steaming up the English Channel on her way back to the UK from the Far East in 1946. On her return she reduced to reserve until refitted for service in the Home Fleet Training Squadron in 1949 with extra mess decks and class rooms built into the former hangars. She was cursed with the same design defects as her sister ship IMPLACABLE and saw no further operational use but spent four years as a training ship based at Portland. In February 1952 she was moored in Dover to act as a saluting ship for members of foreign royal families arriving for the funeral of His Late Majesty King George VI. After a period laid up in the Gareloch, she was sold to the British Iron and Steel Corporation for scrap in September 1956.

(Author's Collection)

HMCS WARRIOR passing through the Miraflores Locks in the Panama Canal in November 1946 for exercises with the Canadian Pacific Fleet. After her return to the RN in 1948 she was used for an unusual series of trials with a 'rubber' flight deck intended to be used by fighters with no undercarriages; making them lighter or allowing more fuel to be carried to improve their performance. Whilst it worked technically with modified Sea Vampires, the weakness of the whole concept was its utter impracticality due to the inability to move the aircraft once it had landed until a crane could lift it onto a wheeled trolley. Landing intervals would have been slow, perhaps five minutes between aircraft compared with under 1 minute for conventional fighters. Worse, a worldwide system of airfields with 'rubber' runways would have been needed for the aircraft to disembark or divert to. After the trials and partial modernisation, WARRIOR was the last British carrier to carry out a patrol off Korea, in 1954, to ensure that the cease-fire was continuing to be correctly observed.

(Ken Kelly)

HM Ships IMPLACABLE and INDEFATIGABLE visited Melbourne in January 1946. The British Pacific Fleet was still a powerful force and carriers visited a number of ports in Australia and New Zealand before returning to the United Kingdom. The sight of three British carriers carrying out a port visit together is unlikely to be repeated. *(Author's Collection)*

74

HMS ILLUSTRIOUS carrying out trials with the Blackburn Firebrand torpedo-fighter in 1946. The aircraft forward is about to be catapulted, the one aft is lined up for free take-off.

(*Syd Goodman Collection*)

HMS ILLUSTRIOUS left the Far East for a refit in Rosyth Dockyard in May 1945. With the end of hostilities, work on her slowed and she did not re-commission until 1946 when she became a trials and training carrier. She is seen here on 27 January 1947 shortly before she had to pay off into reserve due to a lack of manpower. She re-commissioned in September 1948 and spent several valuable years carrying out trials with deck landing the new generation of jet and turbo-prop powered naval aircraft. She saw occasional operational service, ferrying troops to Cyprus during a crisis in the Suez Canal Zone in 1951 and in Exercise 'Mainbrace', the largest NATO maritime exercise ever held, in 1952. Her temporary air group comprised 860 Dutch NAS with Sea Furies and 824 NAS with Fireflies. *(Author's Collection)*

HMS TRIUMPH was launched by Countess Mountbatten of Burma in October 1944 but was not completed until May 1946. While serving with the Mediterranean Fleet in 1947 she embarked King Paul 1 of Greece to witness flying operations by 800 Squadron with Seafires and 827 Squadron with Fireflies. (*Syd Goodman Collection*)

HMS THESEUS taking part in Western Union naval exercises in the Mediterranean on 7 July 1948. She flew the flag of Rear Admiral M J Mansergh who commanded the 3rd Aircraft Carrier squadron and is leading the French aircraft carrier ARRO-MANCHES, her sister ship formerly HMS COLOSSUS, name-ship of their class. In the background, the third ship in line is the submarine depot ship MAIDSTONE.

(Ken Kelly)

HMCS MAGNIFICENT photographed during flying trials off the Isle of Wight on 9 May 1948. She was completed with a normal RN deck recognition letter, 'X' which had previously been allocated to HMS FORMIDABLE, painted on the flight deck but this was replaced with a USN-style 'hull number', '21', when she arrived in Canada. (*Syd Goodman Collection*)

HMS OCEAN on 2 December 1948 during a visit to Naples. Her air group at the time comprised 804 Squadron with Seafires and 812 Squadron with Fireflies. A single Sea Otter amphibian was embarked as a Search and Rescue aircraft for aircrew that had ditched. It is visible with its wings spread just forward of the other aircraft on deck. *(Syd Goodman Collection)*

HMS CAMPANIA was one of a small number of British built escort carriers produced in World War 2. She was used successfully on Russian convoy protection duties with the Home Fleet because it was felt that her riveted hull would be less likely to fracture than the all-welded hulls of American-built ships in the Arctic seas. She is seen here laid up in reserve after a period carrying personnel and stores home from RNAS Piarco in Trinidad during 1945. In 1950 she was converted into a civilian manned exhibition ship to support the Festival of Britain in 1951 by touring British ports. On completion of this duty, she was converted back into an aircraft carrier to act as headquarters ship for the first British atomic bomb tests at Monte Bello Island off North Western Australia. Reduced to reserve again in 1953, she was scrapped in 1955. *(Ken Kelly)*

HMS IMPLACABLE as flagship of the Home Fleet in 1949 firing a gun salute. The light wind is from ahead and is blowing the gun smoke gently astern in clouds that reveal the minute intervals between rounds. (*Author's Collection*)

HMAS SYDNEY moored in Plymouth Sound in February 1949, shortly after her completion by Devonport Dockyard. She arrived in Australia in May of that year but returned to the UK a year later to embark more aircraft for the RAN's Fleet Air Arm.
(*Syd Goodman Collection*)

After a period in the Reserve Fleet, HMS TRIUMPH re-commissioned at Sheerness in 1949 for service in the far East Fleet. She is seen here before leaving the UK with what appear to be motor cars on the flight deck; aircraft carriers were often used to ferry bulky stores and vehicles as well as their aircraft when they deployed to a new station.   (*Syd Goodman Collection*)

HM Australian Ships SYDNEY and WARRAMUNGA arriving in Auckland, New Zealand on 27 March 1950 during combined naval exercises. SYDNEY was another of the 'Majestic' class light fleet carriers sold to Commonwealth navies and, like MAGNIFICENT, was completed largely to the original design. She had commissioned in the UK in 1948 and arrived in Australia in May 1949 with the 20th Carrier Air Group comprising 805 NAS with Sea Furies and 816 NAS with Fireflies. She saw service in the Korean War in 1951/52 but plans to modernise her were cancelled and her days as an aircraft carrier ended in 1958 when she paid off into reserve at Sydney.

(Ken Kelly)

HMS TRIUMPH with the 13th Carrier Air Group embarked, comprising 800 NAS with Seafires and 827 NAS with Fireflies. She was with the Far East Fleet off Japan when the communist North invaded South Korea in June 1950 and was ordered to join Task Force 77 under Vice-Admiral C T Joy USN on 29 June to support UN operations in Korea. The plane-guard destroyer astern is HMS COSSACK and together they joined the USN aircraft carrier VALLEY FORGE to commence strike operations on 3 July. 13 CAG's first target was the enemy airfield at Haeju which was attacked with cannon fire and rockets. On 19 July, TRIUMPH's SAR Sea Otter biplane rescued a ditched USN Corsair pilot from the sea, the last recorded instance in which a RN seaplane carried out an operational rescue.

(Ken Kelly)

HMS UNICORN was a maintenance carrier that had seen extensive service in the Second World War. In June 1950 she was in Singapore Dockyard having delivered a load of aircraft from the UK; she was quickly made ready to sail for Sasebo with aircraft, 300 barrels of rum and other stores to sustain operations by TRIUMPH in the Korean War zone. In August 1950 she embarked men of the Middlesex Regiment from Hong Kong, the first British troops to be deployed to Korea. She is seen here arriving with them on 29 August 1950 in Pusan, the only port under UN control at the time, watched by an American band and other troops. Between 1950 and 1953 UNICORN ferried more than 600 aircraft and 6,000 troops into the war zone. After 1953 she was reduced to reserve in Devonport and, despite plans to bring her back to service after modernisation, she was scrapped in 1959.   (Ken Kelly)

On 18 August 1950 HMS THESEUS sailed from Portsmouth with 17 Carrier Air Group, which had been brought up to war strength, for operations in the Korean War Zone. The Air Group comprised 807 Squadron with Sea Furies and 813 with Fire-flies and was awarded the Boyd Trophy in 1951 for its outstanding operational achievements. She is seen here just after leaving harbour.

(Syd Goodman Collection)

British warships in Sasebo, Japan during the early stage of the Korean War in September 1950. The ships visible in the background, alongside, are HM Ships TRIUMPH and BELFAST, the flagship of Admiral Andrewes, Flag Officer Second-in-Command Far East Station. The ships moored in the foreground are HM Hospital Ship MAINE, HM Ships THESEUS, UNICORN and the armament stores issuing ship RFA FORT ROSALIE. MAINE and UNICORN saw more extensive service during the war than any other Commonwealth vessels.

(*Author's Collection*)

The design of INDOMITABLE was arguably the most successful within the 'Illustrious' group and, other than the re-built VICTORIOUS, she was the only one to see extensive operational service after 1945. The photograph shows her taking part in combined Home and Mediterranean Fleet manoeuvres off Gibraltar in March 1951 with Firebrands and Sea Hornets in the deck park forward. Her large air group at the time comprised 802 NAS with Sea Furies, 820 NAS with Fireflies, 801 and 809 NAS with Sea Hornets, the latter night fighters, and 813 NAS with Firebrands. In 1951 she was the first British carrier to operate a helicopter for plane-guard duties - a Sikorsky S 51 Dragonfly.

(Ken Kelly)

HMS INDOMITABLE on a formal visit to Stockholm on 14 June 1951. As flagship of Admiral Sir Philip Vian the Commander-in-Chief Home Fleet, official visits to European ports formed an important aspect of her duties. Only a very few nations have ever designed, built, equipped and fought with aircraft carriers - Britain, the United States, Japan and, to a lesser extent, France, so the ability to deploy such weapons systems effectively was, and still is, a considerable boost to British prestige abroad.

(Ken Kelly)

HMS EAGLE (2) as originally built with a straight flight deck. She was the first Royal Navy carrier to operate an air group that included jet fighters, the Attackers of 800, 803 and 890 NAS. Unlike the piston-engined types they replaced, the Attackers had no protection in front of the pilot and the steel-wire barriers used until that time were dangerous as they would have crushed the cockpit. A new type of barrier with nylon strands that would let the cockpit through but act on the wings to stop the aircraft had to be introduced before the Attacker could go to sea. In this image, an Attacker is just landing aft and two nylon barriers can just be seen rigged to port of the island. Eight Attackers have already landed and are parked in Fly 1.

(Author's Collection)

The parallel-sided structure on HMS PERSEUS' upper deck is the prototype steam catapult, the BXS-1. This photograph was taken in July 1951 shortly before she sailed to the USA to demonstrate the new catapult to the US Navy. During the trials on both sides of the Atlantic, PERSEUS launched a grand total of over 1,000 dead-loads, some of which were unmanned aircraft with running engines, and 127 piloted aircraft. The aircraft on the catapult is a Sea Hornet and another Sea Hornet, together with a Sturgeon, Skyraider and Avenger are parked aft near the deck-house.

(Syd Goodman Collection)

The 'Colossus' class light fleet carrier POWERFUL was launched by Harland and Wolff on 27 February 1945 but laid up incomplete in Belfast when the Second World War ended. In January 1952 high winds snapped her bow hawsers and blew her across the Victoria Channel, partly blocking the main entrance to the port. It took four tugs to move her back onto her berth and this photograph shows two of them hard at it, the MEADOW and the SOUTHAMPTON. The strength of the wind can be judged from the funnel smoke of the right hand tug. The incident cannot have harmed the ship for, later in the year, she was purchased by the Canadian Government to be completed, eventually, as HMCS BONAVENTURE in 1957.

(Ken Kelly)

HMS WARRIOR was the only 'Colossus' class aircraft carrier to be extensively modernised by the Royal Navy, rather than a foreign navy after sale. The last of her class to complete, she was lent to the Royal Canadian Navy between 1946 and 1948. She is seen here after her first modernisation in 1952 as she appeared when she evacuated 3,000 refugees who sought to escape from the communist regime in North Vietnam to the south in 1954, a humanitarian task for which was awarded a South Vietnamese Presidential Citation. She was modernised again between late 1954 and 1956, emerging with an angled deck, mirror landing aid and improved arrester gear. These were intended to fit her for use as a trials and training carrier but instead she became the flagship for the task force that carried out Operation 'Grapple', the British nuclear tests carried out in the pacific near Christmas Island in 1957. Following the 1957 Defence Review she was declared surplus to requirements and was sold to Argentina in 1958 and re-named INDEPENDENCIA. She was broken up in 1971 after the arrival of 25 de MAYO

(T. Ferrers-Walker)

HMCS MAGNIFICENT entering her home port of Halifax in October 1952 after some months deployed in European waters with the Sea Furies of 871 Squadron and Avengers of 826 Squadron, together comprising 30 Carrier Air Group embarked. (*Syd Goodman Collection*)

After the steam catapult trials, HMS PERSEUS had her upper deck stripped clear and the deck-house aft removed although the crane on the port side forward was retained. She was used as the Royal Navy's first helicopter carrier and as a ferry carrier between 1952 and 1955 during which time she embarked the Whirlwinds of 845 Naval Air Squadron on several occasions to prove the concept of embarked anti-submarine helicopters with considerable success.

(*Syd Goodman Collection*)

A sight unlikely ever to be repeated, the Coronation Review of the Fleet by Her Majesty Queen Elizabeth II on Monday 15 June 1953. There are nine aircraft carriers in the central row, HM Ships EAGLE, INDOMITABLE, IMPLACABLE, INDEFATIGABLE, ILLUSTRIOUS, THESEUS, HMCS MAGNIFICENT, HMAS SYDNEY and the maintenance carrier PERSEUS which was used to provide VIP seating on her flight deck. The sight is all the more impressive when one considers that other operational carriers were deployed in the Mediterranean and Far East Fleets. *(Author's Collection)*

A number of schemes to modernise HMS FORMIDABLE were considered in the late 1940s and early 1950s but they were not proceeded with because of the poor material state the ship was found to be in when she was surveyed. In the event, VICTORIOUS was chosen for modernisation and FORMIDABLE was the first of her class to be sold for scrap. She is seen here soon after her arrival at the breaker's yard at Inverkeithing, an unexpectedly early end for a once-proud ship. *(Ken Kelly)*

Between 1951 and 1953, HMS GLORY carried out more war patrols off the Korean Peninsula than any other British carrier. She is seen here with a range of Sea Furies and Fireflies, each painted with black and white stripes as an allied identification feature, with the first aircraft moving toward the catapult. On 5 May 1953 she equalled the total of 123 sorties in a single day previously achieved by OCEAN. This was a record for a light fleet carrier and involved all squadron pilots flying four sorties and Commander 'Air', the Flight Deck Officer and the 'Batsman' flying two each. Targets included bridges, ox carts and gun positions.

(Author's Collection)

HMS INDOMITABLE alongside in Portsmouth Dockyard. The narrowness of her flight deck aft in this undated image is quite striking and was partially the result of minimising the area of armour plated deck to keep top weight to a minimum. It was also due to the need to contain the deck within the limits bounded by the after 4.5-inch gun mountings to port and starboard as they had to be mounted over sponsons big enough to contain the gun-houses under the turrets and could not be positioned further outboard. The deck of her half-sister VICTORIOUS was widened considerably when she was modernised and had her 4.5-inch guns removed.

(Ken Kelly)

Delays in the completion of HMAS MELBOURNE led the Admiralty to lend VENGEANCE, which was in reserve after service as a ferry carrier, to the RAN in 1952. HMAS VENGEANCE is seen her entering Melbourne with a load of new Sea Furies and Fireflies on 10 March 1953. She was another of the first four light fleet carriers to complete and, like her sisters GLORY, COLOSSUS and VENERABLE had arrived in the British Pacific Fleet just too late for operations against the Japanese. In December 1948 she carried out Operation 'Rusty', a six week cruise in the Arctic to evaluate the effect of extreme cold weather on men, ships and aircraft. Successful flying operations were carried out by aircraft as diverse as Sea Vampire fighters and Dragonfly helicopters.

(Ken Kelly)

HMAS VENGEANCE on 22 July 1953 with Sea Furies of 808 and 850 NAS with Fireflies of 817 NAS ranged on deck. She was returned to the RN on 13 August 1955 with her ship's company manning the new MELBOURNE for the return voyage to Australia. After a period in reserve, she was sold to Brazil in December 1956 and rebuilt in a Dutch shipyard to incorporate the angled deck, steam catapult and mirror landing aid. She was commissioned into the Brazilian Navy on 6 December 1960 as MINAS GERAIS. The original wartime specification for the 'Colossus' class, of which she was one, called for a hull life of three years or the remaining duration of the Second World War. MINAS GERAIS showed how much more capable they were and was not finally broken up until 2004, sixty years after she was launched! *(Author's Collection)*

HMS CENTAUR was the only one of the later light fleet carriers designed in 1943 to be completed to the original design with a straight flight deck. Her sisters were all modified, before completion, with interim angled flight decks. CENTAUR is seen here in October 1953 carrying out initial sea trials in the English Channel, on completion of which she was taken in hand to be fitted with an angled deck before commencing operational service. Note her original flight deck recognition letter 'L'.

(Author's Collection)

A pilot's eye view of ILLUSTRIOUS at recovery stations, steaming fast into wind. The landing signals officer, or batsman, is just visible in the dark area just aft of the port after 4.5 inch gun turret (he would be much more obvious in colour). He is indicating 'slightly high' with his bats. The bow-springs are up, holding the arrester wires clear of the deck but the two barriers abreast the island are un-rigged with their steel wire cables pulled clear of the landing area. The ship is seen as she appeared late in her career as a trials carrier in about 1953 when Y replaced D as her deck recognition letter.

(*Author's Collection*)

HMS INDOMITABLE in 1953 on her return from the Mediterranean Fleet.   (*Syd Goodman Collection*)

HMS ILLUSTRIOUS alongside in Portsmouth Dockyard on 11 November 1954. A dinner was held on board to celebrate the anniversary of the attack on the Italian Fleet at Taranto by Swordfish of 813, 815, 819 and 824 NAS for which they, and IL-LUSTRIOUS, will always be remembered. To mark the occasion, a surviving Swordfish can be seen parked on the after end of the flight deck. The event must have been a sad one because the ship had just carried out her last cruise and was in the process of being de-stored despite only being 14 years old. A month later she was laid up in reserve in the Gareloch with her ship's company being used to man one of the new light fleet carriers. She was sold to the British Iron and Steel Corporation in 1956 and broken up for scrap from 1957.

(Ken Kelly)

A Sea Hawk fighter of 898 NAS being launched from HMS ARK ROYAL (IV) while the ship was moored in Grand Harbour, Malta in December 1956. The mast-head flags and ensign aft show a strong cross-wind from starboard which has affected the aircraft as it left the deck, causing the port wing to drop slightly. The launch shows the enormous potential of the steam catapult to launch aircraft in less than ideal conditions.

(Ken Kelly)

Launch; a Wyvern being catapulted from EAGLE in rough weather. The aircraft has just left the deck as the bow pitches up and the catapult strop is falling away into the sea. Flight deck officers always tried to drop their green flag, ordering the catapult to fire, as the bow dropped so that by the time the aircraft reached the bow it would be pitching up, keeping the aircraft clear of the sea. Failure to get it right could mean the aircraft being launched downwards into the rising swell. In this case the flight deck officer got it right.

(Author's Collection)

Waiting to land on: Sea Hawks of 897 NAS orbit HMS EAGLE in the 'low wait' while other aircraft move up the flight deck to be catapulted. As the launch is completed, the ship will adjust its heading to put the wind down the angled deck rather than the axial deck in line with the catapults. The first aircraft to land will judge its circuit to land on as soon as she is steady. The remaining aircraft in the recovery will aim to back up the first at one minute intervals. *(Author's Collection)*

HMCS MAGNIFICENT was a 'Majestic' class light fleet carrier loaned to Canada by the Royal Navy in 1948. She was completed to the original design and operated an air group which at first comprised 803 NAS with Seafires and 825 NAS with Fireflies. She is seen here leaving Halifax on 29 December 1956 with the Canadian contingent for UN peace-keeping duties in Egypt after the Suez Crisis. This comprised 406 Army personnel, 100 tons of supplies, 233 vehicles, 4 RCAF Otter aircraft and a ship's flight helicopter. The ship's own company had to be reduced to make sufficient accommodation available but the operation shows again the extraordinary versatility of aircraft carriers. MAGNIFICENT was handed back to the Royal Navy in 1957, her ship's company manning the new HMCS BONAVENTURE on her completion. She saw no further operational service and was laid up in the Tamar until 1965 when she was scrapped. *(Ken Kelly)*

A Gannet landing on HMAS MELBOURNE with two further Gannets and a Wessex helicopter parked forward. She was originally laid down for the Royal Navy as the name ship of six 'Majestic' class light fleet carriers which had detail improvements over the original 'Colossus' class. None of the 'Majestics' saw service with the Royal Navy, however, five of them were transferred to Commonwealth navies and one, LEVIATHAN, scrapped incomplete in 1968. MELBOURNE was bought by the Australian Government in 1949 after she had been laid up incomplete for four years. Her completion was delayed to allow incorporation of the major British advances in carrier design, the angled deck, steam catapult and mirror landing aid. She was only the third carrier, after ARK ROYAL and FORRESTAL, in the world to complete with them built in rather than added later.

(Author's Collection)

HMS ARK ROYAL (IV) seen leaving the King George V Dock in Southampton in 1957. The move coincided with a visit by USS FORRESTAL, visible at top right. The ARK's two port forward 4.5-inch gun mountings have been removed to make more space for the angled deck; those to starboard followed a year later. Note the deck edge lift recessed partially into the flight deck. It only served the upper hangar, interfered with flight deck operations and was not considered a success; it was removed during her 1958/59 refit. ARK ROYAL and FORRESTAL were the first two carriers to be completed with the angled deck, steam catapults and the mirror landing aid but the differences between the two ships were striking. ARK ROYAL had a double hangar but smaller flight deck with an interim 5 degree angle. FORRESTAL had a single hangar deck, larger flight deck and a full 8 degree angle requiring a massive port side sponson.
(Ken Kelly)

Amidships detail of HMS ARK ROYAL IV in 1957. The range of aircraft is starting up. The smoke comes from the cartridge starters of the Sea Hawk fighters' Nene engines.
(*Ken Kelly*)

HMS OCEAN leaving Hamburg on 25 June 1957. After brief service as a helicopter carrier during the Suez Crisis in 1956 she returned to duty as a training ship with no aircraft embarked. Friendly visits like this one were an important part of her routine. This had been her third to the famous port.

(Ken Kelly)

HMS ARK ROYAL IV entering New York for a visit after attending an International Naval Review off Hampton Roads in May 1957. The 24 Sea Hawks ranged on deck are from 802, 804 and 898 Squadrons. Visible further aft are Wyverns of 831, Skyraiders of 849B and antisubmarine Gannets of 815 Squadrons.

(*Syd Goodman Collection*)

Aircraft carriers have been put to many uses other than those for which they were designed. ALBION is seen here on 22 July 1958 sailing from Portsmouth with 42 Royal Marines Commando and its vehicles, stores and equipment embarked. They were used to reinforce British forces in the Mediterranean during the Middle East crisis that followed the revolution in Iraq. The Dockyard had to weld over 1,000 extra eye-bolts onto the flight deck so that the vehicles could be securely lashed for the voyage. All of them had to be cut off in Malta Dockyard before her air group could fly out to join her in August when she resumed flying operations. *(Author's Collection)*

On 13 September 1958 the tankers MELIKA and FERNAND GILBERT collided and caught fire in the Gulf of Oman. A British task force including the aircraft carrier BULWARK and the frigate PUMA was in the area and was able to salvage the two stricken ships. BULWARK used the Whirlwind helicopters of 845 NAS to ferry fire-fighting crews under the First Lieutenant across to MELIKA to put out the worst of the fires. The Squadron was subsequently awarded the Boyd Trophy for 1958, awarded to the unit performing the most outstanding feat of naval aviation every year, for its achievement during this salvage operation.

(Author's Collection)

HMS CENTAUR about to launch a range of Sea Hawk fighters. This photograph shows details of her flight deck with the two BH 5 hydraulic catapults forward. The T-shapes at their after end are the rollers of the Catapult Aircraft Line-up Equipment (CALE) gear, intended to move the aircraft main wheels sideways if necessary to line up accurately with the catapult. Aft of them are the jet blast deflectors in the down position either side of the forward lift. CENTAUR was the only ship of her class to complete to the original straight deck design but, after acceptance trials, she was converted to the interim angled deck design seen here.

(Author's Collection)

Despite a number of plans involving the whole class, HMS VICTORIOUS was the only slip of the 'Illustrious' group to be modernised, emerging from Portsmouth Dockyard in 1958 re-boilered and virtually re-built from the hangar deck upwards. Under the terms of the wartime Lend/Lease agreement, the Royal Navy had to reveal its latest technology to the USN for decades after 1945. VICTORIOUS is seen here in New York on a visit in July 1958 after Exercise 'Riptide' which was set up to demonstrate the ship, her Type 984 radar and the associated Comprehensive Display System together with the Scimitar transonic fighter. Although small by USN standards, VICTORIOUS was, at the time, one of the best equipped carriers in existence and the RN was justly proud of her.

(Author's Collection)

In December 1959 HMS CENTAUR visited Brisbane as part of the celebrations to mark the city's centenary. In addition to the ship's company spelling their salute to Brisbane, aircraft in the Alpha Range on deck include the Sea Hawks of 801 NAS, Sea Venoms of 891 NAS and Gannets of 810 NAS. The latter were the last fixed-wing anti-submarine aircraft to deploy in a Royal Navy aircraft carrier.

(Ken Kelly)

HMS ALBION visiting Sydney, New South Wales in 1960. She was the first British carrier to be completed with an interim angled deck and mirror landing aid rather than having them fitted later. This was her final commission as a fixed-wing strike carrier and her air group comprised 806 NAS with Sea Hawks, 894 NAS with Sea Venoms, 815 NAS with Whirlwinds and 849D NAS with Skyraiders. One of the Whirlwinds is on deck, aft of the guard and band on the forward lift.

(Author's Collection)

A Scimitar F1 of 807 NAS seconds after being launched from ARK ROYAL (IV) in Grand Harbour, Malta, on 12 November 1960. This was a more difficult launch than the Sea Hawk four years earlier since the Scimitar was a much heavier aircraft requiring a natural wind which was virtually straight down the deck. The aircraft was flown by Lieutenant Commander 'Jock' Tofts RN, the Commanding Officer and carried just enough fuel for the trip to RNAS Hal Far. Note the Fairey Gannet about to spread its wings on the starboard catapult as the fighter leaves the port catapult.   *(Ken Kelly)*

Landing on; a Sea Vixen FAW 1 seen from the plane guard helicopter seconds before taking a wire on HMS ARK ROYAL (IV). The pilot will have his eyes fixed on the mirror landing aid with occasional glimpses at the runway centre-line to check his line-up. He is nicely positioned with 'four greens' (three wheels and one hook) and flap down. The ship is generating wind over the deck by high speed as there is little natural wind.   *(Author's Collection)*

HMAS MELBOURNE served the RAN well from 1955 to 1982. Throughout that time she showed what could be achieved with a light fleet carrier and, unlike many of her sister ships, she continued to operate a general purpose air group with Skyhawks and Trackers replacing Gannets and Sea Venoms in 1969. As in the UK, attempts to carry forward a replacement carrier programme encountered political opposition, although at one stage the Australian Government were to buy HMS INVINCIBLE, to have been re-named AUSTRALIA, for service in the RAN. Her obvious importance in the South Atlantic War in 1982, however, led the British Government to ask for the deal to be cancelled.

(Ken Kelly)

In December 1957 HMS OCEAN completed her last cruise as a training ship and returned to Devonport Dockyard to be de-stored. Although she was only twelve years old and had seen the world's first deck landing by a jet fighter followed by an impressive war record in Korea, she was to see no further service and was towed away to be scrapped at Faslane on 6 May 1962. She is seen here, stripped of all useful equipment, laid up in the River Tamar in 1961. *(Author's Collection)*

On 29 June 1961 HMS VICTORIOUS was serving with the Far East Fleet on route from Singapore to Hong Kong when she was ordered to the Persian Gulf with all despatch to defend Kuwait against a threatened Iraqi invasion. In the meantime, BULWARK arrived with 42 Royal Marines Commando and the Whirlwind helicopters of 848 NAS embarked. When VICTORIOUS arrived on station some days later, she was able to take on the air defence of Kuwait with her sophisticated radar and Sea Vixen fighters. The Scimitars stood ready to attack Iraqi ground forces should it become necessary. The threatened invasion did not materialise when the Iraqi leader realised that he would have to attack British forces to achieve his aim and it can fairly be said that the prompt action taken by the Royal Navy's carrier task groups averted a war.

(Author's Collection)

HMS ARK ROYAL (IV) anchored in Buckner Bay, Okinawa after the combined RN/USN Exercise 'Rawfish' in February 1962. The air group comprised 800 NAS with Scimitars, 890 NAS with Sea Vixens, 815 NAS with Wessex and 849C with Gannet AEW aircraft. There was also a COD Gannet, visible between a Scimitar and AEW Gannet in Fly 1, the deck space forward of the island.

(Ken Kelly)

HMAS SYDNEY began a second 'life' in 1961 when she was converted into a fast troop transport with extra accommodation built into the former hangar, new cranes and extra lashing points for vehicles on the flight deck. She retained the ability to operate helicopters and, like the British commando carriers, she was modified to carry utility landing craft on davits. Between 1965 and 1972 she carried 16,094 troops; 5,753 tons of cargo; 2,375 vehicles and 14 aircraft to and from Vietnam. In that period she steamed 345,000 miles; 80,000 of them in 1971. After this striking demonstration of another use to which this form of vessel can be put, she was paid off into reserve as an economy measure in 1973 and broken up for scrap in South Korea in 1975.

(Author's Collection)

HMS VICTORIOUS turning at high speed and, to judge from the funnel smoke, still accelerating. Her modernisation in Portsmouth Dockyard lasted longer and cost more than a new aircraft carrier would have done but the Admiralty could not have known that when work started in 1950. Many of the vital improvements, including the angled flight deck, steam catapults, mirror landing aid and Type 984 radar only became available after the original work had started and it would have made no sense to complete her without them. She was the first warship in the Royal Navy to deploy with nuclear weapons, the 'Red Beard' tactical bomb carried at the time by Scimitars but eventually capable of use by Sea Vixens and Buccaneers as well. The aircraft on deck are Mark 1 Buccaneers and Sea Vixens with two Gannet AEW 3 aft of the island. The tractor teams are moving aircraft from the forward part of the deck (Fly 1) where they were parked after landing to the range aft (Fly 3) where they will be prepared for launch. *(Author's Collection)*

HMS VICTORIOUS photographed berthed in Yokosuka, Japan with other units of the Far East Fleet on 14 May 1964. The aircraft visible on deck are a Buccaneer S1 of 801 NAS and a Sea Vixen of 893 NAS. Buccaneers were invariably parked with their air-brakes open as this shortened the aircraft for stowage in tight spots. Note the significant overhang of the flight deck compared with the earlier image of INDOMITABLE showing that VICTORIOUS benefited from better deck design as did all the other improvements in her modernisation. The modernised EAGLE was the only British carrier that could claim to have been better than VICTORIOUS in the 90 year history of the type. *(Ken Kelly)*

In January 1964 units of the Tanganyikan Army mutinied and Britain was asked to help the Government to restore order. CENTAUR was at Aden and, in addition to her air group was able to embark 45 Royal Marines Commando with ammunition stores and some vehicles together with the 16/5 Lancers, their armoured cars and two RAF Belvedere helicopters. The military vehicles can be seen here on the starboard side of the flight deck forward, allowing the port catapult to be used to launch aircraft. Most aircraft had to stay on deck as the Marines used the hangar as a mess deck. After a fast passage to the scene of operations, the Wessex helicopters were used to land Marines in a surprise dawn assault with complete success showing how flexible aircraft carriers can be. If necessary, the fighters could have been catapulted but the Belvederes would have to have got airborne to recover them, an evolution called 'Plan Squeeze'.

(Author's Collection)

HMCS BONAVENTURE moving alongside Jetty 4, her home berth, at HM Canadian Dockyard Halifax in November 1965 with destroyer escorts ahead of her on jetties 2 and 3. She was originally laid down as the 'Majestic' class carrier POWERFUL for the Royal Navy in November 1943 and launched in February 1945 but laid up incomplete when World War 2 ended. She was purchased by the Canadian Government in 1952 for completion to a revised and very improved design and commissioned in 1957. She was, to date, the only aircraft carrier owned outright by the Canadians but was prematurely scrapped as a cost saving measure in 1971 when she still had decades of potential life ahead of her. *(Author's Collection)*

HMS CENTAUR leaving Liverpool after a formal visit. The Alpha Range includes the Sea Vixens of 892 NAS, the Gannet AEW 3s of 849A NAS and the Wessex helicopters of 815 NAS. Despite being refitted with steam rather than hydraulic catapults and other improvements in 1957, CENTAUR had a surprisingly short operational life of only eleven years from 1954 to 1965. She paid off into reserve in December 1965 to act as an accommodation ship for other carriers in refit, first in Portsmouth then Plymouth. She was sold to ship breakers in Kent for scrap in 1972. *(T. Ferrers-Walker)*

EAGLE was completely re-built between 1958 and 1964, emerging with steam catapults, a fully an-gled flight deck, projector landing aid and Type 984 air warning radar. She is seen here moving away from the wall in Singapore Dockyard while serving with the Far East Fleet in 1965. To the left is the Stores Basin which is still owned by the UK Ministry of Defence. The area in front of the Red House, where this photograph was taken is now a restaurant and the Dockyard is a commercial shipyard. The aircraft visible on deck are Buccaneers and Wessex helicopters. *(Author's Collection)*

Exercise 'FOTEX 65' was one of the largest Commonwealth naval exercises ever carried out and brought together ships of the RN, RAN, RNZN and Royal Malaysian Navy in the South China Sea. Four aircraft carriers formed the core of the assembled fleet; HMS BULWARK, HMAS MELBOURNE and HMS VICTORIOUS are seen here in line astern of HMS EAGLE.

(Author's Collection)

Trials with a Hawker P 1127 prototype V/STOL fighter were carried out on HMS BULWARK in June 1966 to investigate the possibility of operating developed versions of the type from small carriers. Note the white line painted along the original angled deck centreline from the ship's days as a fixed-wing carrier. The P1127 is halfway through a successful rolling take-off and, as soon as it is clear the Wessex HU 5 helicopters on the starboard side forward will be ranged for a quick take-off. They already have their port engines running and tractors attached to their tailwheels ready to pull them aft onto numbered spots. The trials deliberately looked into the potential problems of operating both helicopters and V/STOL jets and proved that they could operate together remarkably successfully. (*Author's Collection*)

HMS LEVIATHAN was launched on 7 June 1945 but never completed. She was a unit of the Majestic class and was built by Swan Hunter on the Tyne. With the end of the Second World War there was no immediate need for her and she was laid up incomplete in Fareham Creek in July 1946. Between 1950 and 1958 she was used as a spare gear store and accommodation ship for dockyard personnel in Portsmouth working on the re-construction of VICTORIOUS. During that time she was improperly preserved and although plans were considered to complete her as a commando carrier or missile cruiser, none came to fruition. In 1966 her boilers and turbines were removed by Portsmouth Dockyard and sold to the Dutch shipyard that refitted KAREL DOORMAN (formerly HMS VENERABLE) for sale to Argentina. After many years anchored in Fareham Creek she was towed to Faslane and broken up in 1968. *(Author's Collection)*

To keep the name HERMES alive, a light fleet carrier laid down as ELEPHANT in 1944 was re-named in 1945 when another unit of the class, to have been named HERMES, was cancelled. She was a half sister to ALBION, BULWARK and CENTAUR but completed five years later with a fully angled flight deck, steam catapults, mirror landing aid, side lift and Type 984 three-dimensional search radar. She was launched in 1953 by the wife of the Prime Minister, Mrs Winston Churchill and although small, she was one of the best equipped aircraft carriers in the world when she was eventually completed in 1959. She formed part of the Far East Fleet when this photograph was taken, her air group comprising 801 NAS with Buccaneers, 893 NAS with Sea Vixens, 849A NAS with Gannets and 814 NAS with Wessex. *(Author's Collection)*

HMS HERMES leaving Garden Island Dockyard after a successful visit to Sydney in 1968 with the destroyer GLAMORGAN astern. The visit had started after Exercise 'Coral Sands' on 14 October with warships of four navies comprising the largest fleet to enter the harbour since World War 2. The author was serving in HERMES at the time to gain watch-keeping and ocean navigation certificates and can be seen in charge of the guard, visible inboard of the side lift. She was one of the last carriers to be stationed permanently east of Suez.

(Author's Collection)

HMS HERMES (2) taking part in a four ship Replenishment at Sea while serving with the Far East Fleet. From left to right the ships are the Daring class destroyer DIANA, a Tide class RFA tanker, HERMES and the RFA air stores support ship RELIANT. Note that the side lift is down allowing stores to be taken directly into the hangar and struck down rather than having to be dumped first onto the flight deck as in other carriers. *(Author's Collection)*

HMS EAGLE off Cape Town; note the cloud forming a 'cloth' over Table Mountain. Hands have just fallen in for a ceremonial harbour entry and aircraft are in an Alpha Range on the flight deck. After her modernisation, EAGLE's air group comprised the Buccaneers of 800 NAS, Sea Vixens of 899 NAS, Gannets of 849D NAS and Wessex of 820 NAS.

(Author's Collection)

HMS ARK ROYAL (IV) as she appeared during the filming of the BBC TV series 'Sailor'. She is carrying out a Replenishment at Sea (RAS) with the tanker OLMEDA to starboard and the stores ship LYNESS to port. By this stage her air group was the most powerful ever deployed by the Royal Navy with the Phantoms of 892 NAS, Buccaneers of 809 NAS, Gannets of 849B NAS and Sea Kings of 824 NAS. The projection at the bow was a 'strop-catcher' which allowed the wire strops used to hook the aircraft to the steam catapult shuttle to be used several times rather than being lost into the sea on every launch.

(Author's Collection)

ARK ROYAL (IV) being towed from Devonport to the breaker's yard at Cairnryan on 22 September 1980 watched by a sad crowd on Plymouth Hoe. The smoke came from burning mattresses put into the funnel by the towing party to make it look as if she was steaming! At the time it was thought that she would be the Royal Navy's last strike carrier but subsequent events showed how indispensable such ships are to the nation and the 'Invincible' class have undergone a role change from anti-submarine to strike carriers, albeit on a smaller scale than their predecessors. In 1998 the British Government an-nounced that a new class of aircraft carriers, larger than ARK ROYAL were to be built.

(T. Ferrers-Walker)

A weather-worn HMS HERMES being joined by the new ILLUSTRIOUS on her return from the South Atlantic in 1982. After modification with a ski-jump to operate Sea Harriers, she had played a key role in the liberation of the Falkland Islands with Sea Harriers of 800, 809 and 899 NAS embarked together with Sea Kings of 826 and 846 NAS. They were joined later by 1 Squadron RAF with its Harriers. HERMES had spent 108 days at sea, a record only broken by INVINCIBLE in the same conflict. She was sold to the Indian Navy in 1986 and re-named VIRAAT. At the time of writing, she is still in service.

(Author's Collection)

HMS ARK ROYAL (5) in 1984, a year before her completion. She is alongside Swan Hunter's Walker Naval Yard on the Tyne. She was the last of a long line of famous warships to be built there and shortly after she sailed in June 1985 the shipyard was demolished except for the 'hammerhead' crane. Note the grey 'boot-topping' paint introduced after the South Atlantic War but discarded shortly afterwards.

(*Author's collection*)

HMS ARK ROYAL (V), still flying the red ensign, seen entering her new base port at Portsmouth for the first time on 1 July 1985. She had left Swan Hunter's Walker Naval Yard on the Tyne on 28 June with a Swordfish embarked, seen here at the after end of the flight deck. It was joined by a Sea Harrier of 899 NAS, parked on the ski-jump, for the ceremonial entry. Note the fly-past by three Sea Kings immediately over the ship and the crowds on the Round Tower and other vantage points. After trials and a shake-down cruise, she was commissioned by Her Majesty Queen Elizabeth, The Queen Mother on 1 November 1985 in Portsmouth.

(Author's Collection)

With six Sea Harrier F/A 2 and six Harrier GR 7 fast-jets ranged on deck together with four Sea King helicopters parked close against the island, this aerial photograph of HMS INVINCIBLE in September 1997 shows the latent capability this class always had to operate STOVL strike fighters in significant numbers. An air group of three Sea King AEW helicopters and eighteen Sea Harriers was possible although magazine capacity would have been an issue in continuous operations. (*MoD/Crown Copyright*)

HMS ILLUSTRIOUS seen operating in company with the USS JOHN C STENNIS, CVN 74, in 1998. Although small by comparison with the big USN aircraft carrier, she has eight Sea Harriers, five harriers and two Sea King helicopters on deck, a significant package of tactical air power by the standards of most nations. (*MoD/Crown Copyright*)

In 2008 HMS ARK ROYAL (V) operated as an amphibious assault helicopter carrier while the LPH OCEAN was in refit; note the Amphibious Warfare Squadron badge on the forward funnel. As such she had no dedicated air group but operated an 'ad hoc' force of helicopters to support Royal Marines Commandos in exercises and on stand-by for operations. She had previously operated as an LPH during the Gulf War of 2003 when her helicopters landed Marines to capture the Al Faw Peninsula. A third, or 'mizzen' mast has been added to the ship to cope with the extra communications equipment fitted to the ship to enable her to act as a task force flagship.

(*Michael Nitz - Naval Press Service*)

A computer generated image of how the new HMS QUEEN ELIZABETH, for which a construction contract was signed in July 2008, will appear after completion. The aircraft depicted are F-35B Lightning II Joint Strike Fighters and a single Merlin helicopter but she is likely to have to operate Harriers from her planned completion date in 2014 until 2018.
(BVT Shipbuilders)

INDEX